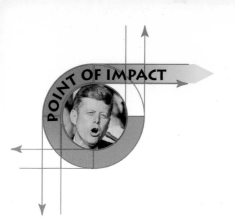

POINT OF IMPACT

The Assassination of John F. Kennedy

Death of the New Frontier

KAREN PRICE HOSSELL

Chicago, Illinois

Designed by Roslyn Broder
Printed in the United States by Lake Book Manufacturing, Inc.

07 06 05 04 03
10 9 8 7 6 5 4 3 2 1

Library of Congress Cataloging-in-Publication Data
Price Hossell, Karen, 1957-
   The assassination of John F. Kennedy : death of the New Frontier / by
Karen Price Hossell.
        p. cm. -- (Point of impact)
Summary: Provides an overview of John Kennedy's presidency, describes
the events surrounding his assassination, and discusses its impact on
the American people and American society.
   ISBN 1-58810-905-4 (HC), 1-40340-533-6 (Pbk)
   I. Kennedy, John F. (John Fitzgerald), 1917-1963--Assassination [1.
Kennedy, John F. (John Fitzgerald), 1917-1963--Assassination.] I.
Title. II. Series.
   E842.9 .P75 2002
   973.922'092--dc21
                                    2001008694

Acknowledgments
The author and publishers are grateful to the following for permission to reproduce copyright material:
pp. 4, 7, 8, 9, 14, 15, 20, 21, 22, 23, 25, 26 Bettmann/Corbis; pp. 5, 10, 17 Corbis; p. 6 Flip Schulke/Corbis; pp. 11, 16, 18 AP/Wide World Photos; p. 12 Hulton-Deutsch Collection/Corbis; p. 19 William A. Bake/Corbis; p. 27 Wally McNamee/Corbis; p. 28 NASA; p. 29 Rob Rowan, Progressive Image/Corbis.

Cover photograph by (T-B): Bettmann/Corbis; AP/Wide World Photos.

Every effort has been made to contact copyright holders of any material reproduced in this book. Any omissions will be rectified in subsequent printings if notice is given to the publisher.

The author would like to thank her parents, her husband, David, and her editor, Angela McHaney Brown.

Some words are shown in bold, **like this.** You can find out what they mean by looking in the glossary.

Contents

The Murder of a President

On November 21, 1963, President John Fitzgerald Kennedy and his wife, Jacqueline, flew to Texas. With them were the Vice President and former Texas senator Lyndon B. Johnson and his wife. They went to San Antonio and Fort Worth, then flew to Dallas on November 22. The president was scheduled to speak there at a luncheon.

President and Mrs. Kennedy rode to the luncheon in a convertible with Texas governor John B. Connally and his wife. A limousine full of **Secret Service** agents rode behind them for protection, and Vice President and Mrs. Johnson rode in another limousine behind that car. The cars formed a sort of parade called a motorcade.

People lined the streets of Dallas, Texas, to see the handsome president and glamorous first lady.

Tragedy strikes

Kennedy smiled and waved at the crowd as the motorcade slowly drove through the streets of Dallas. Then the president suddenly grabbed his neck and leaned over as though he was in pain. Seconds later, he fell into his wife's lap. The crowd did not know what had happened, but the driver of the president's limousine and the cars following it sped up and raced away.

The president had been shot twice—once in the neck and once in the head—and Governor Connally, who was sitting in front of the president, had also been shot. The limousine picked up speed as the driver raced to Parkland Hospital. The president's injuries were too severe, however, and doctors could do nothing to save him. At one o'clock—30 minutes after he was shot—the president was pronounced dead. Governor Connally was badly injured as well, but he survived.

The news spreads

All over the country, people heard the news. Wives called their husbands at work to tell them the president had been shot. Teachers were called into hallways, then went back into the classroom to tell their students the sad news. Then more news came. Television stations interrupted regular programming to announce that President Kennedy was dead.

Many people across the world felt their lives were changed forever by the assassination of President Kennedy.

The country and the world were shocked. The 46-year-old president and father of two young children was gone. Schools let their students go home early. People sobbed in the streets. Even Walter Cronkite, a man millions of Americans had watched deliver the news on television for years and had never seen cry, had to hold back tears as he delivered the news to the country. For a day, everything stopped. When things started up again, they would never be the same. Historically, Kennedy's **assassination** marks a passage from a time of innocence and wealth to a time of **unrest** and increased awareness of social problems.

The Times

The 1950s were a time of economic success for many Americans. After World War II ended in 1945, many veterans went to college, got married, and had children. More affordable homes were being built, and new technology was making life easier for everyone. Most women did not work outside the home in the 1950s, and they had new appliances to make their housework easier, including dishwashers, air conditioners, and sewing machines. In the evenings, families gathered around the television to watch programs about happy, middle-class families.

Martin Luther King Jr., a 27-year-old activist, led a bus **boycott** in Montgomery, Alabama, in 1956 to protest segregation in transportation.

Inequality

Not everyone lived this way, though. African Americans were rarely on television or in movies in the 1950s. People were **segregated**—separated by race—in many areas of life, including schools and public transportation.

In 1954, the United States **Supreme Court** ruled in the court case *Brown v. Board of Education* that it was **unconstitutional** to segregate students in public schools. Schools were told to begin to **desegregate,** but many whites violently protested this.

The Cold War

The United States had problems at home such as racial **unrest,** but the country also had to face the worldwide problem of the **Cold War.** This was not an actual war but, rather, a conflict of politics and other ideas of government between the two great powers in the world.

One power was the United States and its allies, or friends, called the West. The other was the **Soviet Union** and its allies, called the East. The Cold War began when World War II ended in 1945.

The main reason for the conflict between countries was their differing ideas of how a nation should be governed. The Soviet Union believed that **communism** was the best way to run a country, while the United States was—and still is—a **democracy.** Each power feared attack from the other, and each country also feared the other was planning to take over other countries. As a result of these fears, both the United States and the Soviet Union built up their stock of nuclear weapons.

Led by Cold War fears, some Americans built bomb shelters as a place to hide in the event of a nuclear bomb attack.

BLACKLISTING

In the 1950s and 1960s, fear of communism led to the persecution of Americans merely suspected of being sympathetic to communism. Many people, including Hollywood writers, movie and television stars, college professors, and people in labor unions, were accused of being communist or of attending communist meetings. After the accusations, they became blacklisted. That meant that their names were published in newspapers and mentioned in gossip on the streets and in company meetings. Many employers refused to hire blacklisted persons.

John F. Kennedy

John F. Kennedy was born in Brookline, Massachusetts, in 1917. Both sides of his family were involved in politics. His father's father was a state senator. His mother's father, John F. Fitzgerald, was a state senator, a United States Congressman, and the mayor of Boston. Kennedy's father, Joseph P. Kennedy, was a U.S. **ambassador** to Great Britain and businessman who became a millionaire.

War hero

John F. Kennedy graduated from Harvard University in 1940. He joined the U.S. Navy during World War II and was assigned to a PT boat, or patrol torpedo—a small, fast fighting ship. In August 1943, his boat was patrolling off the Solomon Islands in the South Pacific when it was cut in two by a Japanese ship. Two men were killed, and the ten other men on board, including Kennedy, clung to wreckage all night. The next morning, they sighted an island, and Kennedy ordered everyone to swim to it. Even though Kennedy's back was badly injured, he helped another injured man swim to the island. They were rescued several days later. Kennedy received a Navy and Marine Corps Medal for his heroism and a Purple Cross for being wounded in combat.

Kennedy took command of the patrol boat *PT 109* on April 23, 1943.

Public figure

After the war, Kennedy ran for the U.S. House of Representatives and won. He served as a Democratic congressman for Massachusetts from 1947 to 1952. In 1952, he ran for and won a seat in the U.S. Senate.

Kennedy's wartime back injury began to bother him more and more, though, so he had surgery in both

1954 and 1955. While he was recovering from surgery, Kennedy wrote a book called *Profiles in Courage*. For the book, he won the 1957 Pulitzer Prize—an important American award given to only a few writers each year.

Presidential campaign

In 1956, Kennedy decided to run for president in the 1960 election. Many people thought it would be a problem that Kennedy was a Roman Catholic. Only one other Roman Catholic had ever been **nominated** for president, and he lost the election. Some people also thought Kennedy was too young. If he won, he would become president at age 43, making him the youngest person ever to be president. His Republican opponent was Richard M. Nixon, who had been vice president for eight years under Dwight D. Eisenhower and was associated with the wartime generation.

Kennedy was nominated at the 1960 Democratic National Convention to run for president. His youthful energy and ideals appealed to a new generation of voters.

A FUTURE OF CHALLENGES

As Kennedy **campaigned** for president, he put together a program he called "The New Frontier." Kennedy accepted the Democratic Party's nomination for president by making a speech about his goals for the New Frontier. The following is from his speech:

We stand today on the edge of a New Frontier—the frontier of the 1960s—a frontier of unknown opportunities and perils—a frontier of unfulfilled hopes and threats. . . . But the New Frontier of which I speak is not a set of promises—it is a set of challenges. It sums up not what I intend to offer the American people, but what I intend to ask of them. . . . But I tell you the New Frontier is here, whether we seek it or not. Beyond that frontier are the uncharted areas of science and space, unsolved problems of peace and war, unconquered pockets of ignorance and prejudice, unanswered questions of poverty and surplus.

The New Frontier

The 1960 debates

In 1960, Kennedy decided to use television in a way no other presidential candidate had. He challenged Richard M. Nixon to a series of four televised **debates.** Nixon's advisers told him not to do it, because he was ahead in the polls and was expected to win the election anyway. He wanted to debate Kennedy, though, so he agreed to go on television.

Kennedy is shown here with the man monitoring his debate with Nixon.

On the night of the first debate, Nixon was pale and thin, because he had just spent time in the hospital recovering from a knee injury. He also had what is called a five-o'clock shadow—his face looked unshaven even though he had just shaved. On the other hand, Kennedy was tan and healthy looking. During the debates he appeared cool and confident, while Nixon was sweaty and seemed nervous. Those who heard the debates on the radio thought Nixon did a better job, but those who saw them on television pronounced Kennedy the winner. And indeed, he did go on to win the election—by about only 120,000 **popular votes.**

The New Frontier platform

Kennedy's "New Frontier" **platform** had many goals. They included a higher **minimum wage,** medical care for the elderly, increased **federal** aid for education, **legislation** for **civil rights,** improved life in cities, and major tax cuts. Kennedy also wanted to "win" the **Cold War** by spending more money on weapons. The goals of increased minimum wage and increased spending on weapons were achieved, but many of his other goals were not. One reason was that **Congress** was not ready to pass some of his **reforms.** Another reason was that he did not push to get legislation passed, particularly legislation about civil rights.

Kennedy planned to prepare Congress for his new ideas during his first presidential term so that when he ran again—and won—in 1964, his reforms would be passed. To be reelected, Kennedy would need the votes of Southern Democrats, and many in the South were against civil rights. Most of the time he was in office, President Kennedy tried to **enforce** civil rights laws already in place.

Neighborhoods such as this street in New York were part of the focus of Kennedy's New Frontier. He wanted to reduce poverty levels and bring up the standard of living for many Americans.

A CALL TO SERVICE

On January 20, 1961, the day of his **inauguration,** President Kennedy spoke these words in his speech. He called upon his audience to help make the world a better place:

In your hands, my fellow citizens, more than in mine, will rest the final success or failure of our course. Since this country was founded, each generation of Americans has been summoned to give testimony to its national loyalty. The graves of young Americans who answered the call to service surround the globe. Now the trumpet summons us again—not as a call to bear arms, though arms we need; not as a call to battle, though embattled we are—but a call to bear the burden of a long twilight struggle, year in and year out, 'rejoicing in hope, patient in tribulation'—a struggle against the common enemies of man: tyranny, poverty, disease, and war itself.

The 35th President

The Peace Corps

One of Kennedy's first actions after becoming president was to create the Peace Corps. This organization came to represent his "New Frontier." The goal of the Peace Corps is to promote world peace and friendship. Volunteers help in areas such as education, healthcare, and technology—whatever is needed by a country. To promote more understanding between countries, they learn how other people live and show those people how Americans live.

The Peace Corps is still active, and more than 150,000 Americans have been volunteers. To many Americans, the Peace Corps was a promise of more things to come while Kennedy was president. The promise was cut short by Kennedy's assassination.

Fidel Castro was the leader of Cuba at the time of both the Bay of Pigs invasion and the Cuban Missile Crisis.

The Bay of Pigs invasion

Kennedy was forced to deal with two incidents involving Cuba while he was president. The first incident was the Bay of Pigs invasion, which took place in April 1961. The U.S. **Central Intelligence Agency (CIA)** had trained Cuban **exiles**—people who had left Cuba to live in the United States—to overthrow Cuba's **communist** government.

Unfortunately, the invasion did not go as planned. Cuban airplanes bombed American ships, and CIA boats wrecked on a coral reef. Local Cubans were there to meet the invaders when they landed and held them until the Cuban army arrived. About 1,100 of the 1,400 invaders were captured, and 114 died.

The Cuban Missile Crisis

In October 1962, there was another problem in Cuba. U.S. spy planes flying over Cuba saw missile sites being set up with missiles aimed at the United States. The plane photographed the sites and U.S. intelligence agencies studied the photographs. The agencies soon verified that Cuba and the **Soviet Union** were setting up nuclear missiles in Cuba. Kennedy and his advisers thought long and hard about this **Cold War** threat to the United States. They considered an air strike or an invasion, but finally settled on a **naval blockade** of Cuba. Ships from the U.S. Navy surrounded the island country and stopped any other ships from going in or coming out.

The United States and the Soviet Union finally settled the issue in November 1962. Kennedy agreed not to invade Cuba and to withdraw U.S. missiles from Turkey, a country near the Soviet Union. Nikita S. Khrushchev, the leader of the Soviet Union, then agreed to remove Soviet missiles from Cuba. Kennedy's skillful handling of the situation raised his reputation internationally.

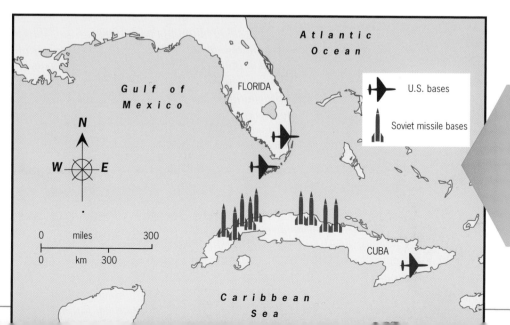

U.S. bases

Soviet missile bases

Cuba was a serious threat to the United States because it was so close to Florida.

13

Civil Rights and the Cold War

Because the **Cold War** was such an important issue during the late 1950s and early 1960s, Kennedy did not focus much attention on the issue of **civil rights.** But trouble had been brewing in the country for years over racial differences, especially in the South. In 1955 in Montgomery, Alabama, Rosa Parks refused to sit in the back of the bus as African Americans were supposed to do. Her action led to a bus **boycott** headed by Martin Luther King Jr. In 1957, King formed the Southern Christian Leadership Conference, which worked for change using nonviolent means.

Taking a stand

In 1960, four African-American men staged what was called a sit-in at a local lunch counter in Greensboro, North Carolina. Because they were black, they were not supposed to sit at the counter, and no one would serve them. They refused to move, however, and sat there for about two hours while white customers were served. More sit-ins took place throughout the South. Then a group of seven African Americans and six white people took a "Freedom Ride" through the South. Their goal was to break down **segregation** in the national transportation system. The group was attacked by a mob in Rock Hill, South Carolina, and the bus was set on fire just inside the Alabama border. Other groups took freedom rides and met with more violence.

Rosa Parks set progress in motion by taking a brave stand against racism.

These events made President Kennedy turn his attention to the issue of civil rights. After more violence, including the bombing of a Birmingham, Alabama, church in which four African-American girls were killed, he wrote **legislation** that focused on civil rights. The civil rights bill banned racial **discrimination** in public places, prohibited employers and labor unions from discriminating against employees because of race, and denied **federal** funds to segregated schools.

LIMITED NUCLEAR TEST BAN TREATY

Because of the Cold War, the United States and the **Soviet Union** tested nuclear bombs in the air, underground, and under water. When the bombs and missiles were tested, they would cause dangerous **radioactive fallout.** President Eisenhower tried to form an agreement with the Soviet Union to stop the testing. He and Soviet leader Nikita Khrushchev agreed to stop, but no formal agreement was signed. In September 1960, the Soviet Union began testing bombs again, despite the agreement. When President Kennedy discovered this, he allowed the United States to start testing also. After the Cuban Missile Crisis, the two countries decided to stop the tests. In July 1963, the countries reached a formal agreement to stop testing nuclear weapons.

U.S. troops gathered to watch an atomic bomb explode at a test site. Such tests greatly concerned the public.

One Day in Dallas

On November 22, 1963, many people in Dallas, Texas, were excited about President Kennedy's visit there as part of his political tour. Downtown, people stopped working to go out to the street or look out the window to see the president's motorcade drive by. They took pictures to show their children and grandchildren that they had seen the president.

Many Kennedy supporters gathered to greet John and Jackie Kennedy at the Dallas airport.

Not everyone was happy that the president was coming to Texas, however. Some people did not like the fact that he came from a wealthy family. The president, they thought, did not understand what poor people had to go through. Some did not like the president's views on **civil rights.** They preferred that African Americans live, eat, shop, and go to school separately, rather than with white people. But even though some people disagreed with Kennedy's politics, most of them wished the president no harm. They knew he had been a hero in World War II, and they respected his role as president.

The Assassin

At least one man, though, was there that day specifically to harm President Kennedy. His name was Lee Harvey Oswald, and he had stationed himself at a window in the fifth floor of the Texas School Book Depository building where he worked. As Kennedy's motorcade drove by, Oswald shot the president using a high-powered rifle. Later that day, Oswald was walking down the street near the boardinghouse where he lived when a police officer stopped his car, got out, and began to question him. The **assassin** shot and killed the police officer, then ran into a movie theater to hide. Officers found him there and arrested him.

Two days later, as Oswald was being moved from one jail to another, a man named Jack Ruby stepped out of a crowd of reporters and shot him. Oswald died soon afterward. Ruby said he killed Oswald because he did not want Jacqueline Kennedy to have to sit through a court trial. Many people, however, think Ruby and Oswald were connected, and that Ruby killed Oswald to keep him quiet.

This photograph of Oswald with his rifle was taken in his backyard sometime before the Kennedy **assassination.**

THE END OF CAMELOT

The new president and first lady fascinated even those who were not interested in politics. Some people said that the Kennedy days in the White House were like Camelot—the legendary kingdom of King Arthur—because everything was beautiful and everyone was happy. The Kennedys seemed as much like a king and queen as they did the president and first lady. They came from wealthy families, went to the best schools, wore expensive designer clothes, and had famous friends, many of them movie stars. American women watched closely to see what Jackie Kennedy was wearing, and she often started trends in fashion. When Kennedy was killed, this magic time was shattered.

After the Assassination

Vice President Johnson was at the hospital when President Kennedy was pronounced dead. As soon as they heard the news, **Secret Service** agents rushed Johnson and his wife back to the presidential airplane to protect him. About an hour later, Mrs. Kennedy came to the airplane with her husband's body, which had been sealed in a coffin. A **federal** judge, Sarah Hughes, came to the airplane and swore the Vice President into office. Lyndon B. Johnson was now president of the United States.

The funeral

A funeral was held for John F. Kennedy on November 25, 1963. A horse-drawn cart pulled his casket through the streets of Washington, D.C., on its way to the funeral mass at St. Matthew's Cathedral. A riderless horse, the symbol of a fallen warrior who would never ride again, walked alongside the cart.

Heads of state, including kings, presidents, prime ministers, and other representatives from 92 nations came to Kennedy's funeral.

The presidents of France, Germany, Israel, and Korea attended, as did leaders from Turkey, Canada, Greece, Great Britain, Belgium, and the Netherlands.

John F. Kennedy was buried at Arlington National Cemetery in Virginia. On his grave is an "eternal flame," a symbol Jacqueline had placed there to remind the world that he gave his life for his country. Fueled by an underground line of natural gas, the flame at Kennedy's grave always burns.

WORDS OF SORROW

Members of the president's staff were deeply saddened by his death. Robert McNamara, the secretary of defense during both the Kennedy and Johnson administrations, said of John F. Kennedy's death that the country *"had suffered a loss which it would take ten years to repair"* and that there was *"no one on the horizon to compare with the President as our national leader."* Averell Harriman, who was assistant secretary of state for Far Eastern affairs, said Kennedy's influence was much like that of Franklin D. Roosevelt, who had been president from 1932 to 1945. Harriman said, *"No two presidents before had had world opinion and affection centered upon them as had Roosevelt and Kennedy. In both cases people abroad felt they had lost a personal friend."*

The World Reacts

In the days after the **assassination,** the people of the United States tried to understand what had happened. For days, television networks focused on coverage of the president's death and his funeral. They also played clips from his life, taken from Kennedy home movies, the home movies of his friends, and newsreels the networks had on file.

People waited in line for hours to pay their respects at the grave of a beloved president.

Americans were not alone in their grief. All over the world, people mourned President Kennedy's death. When news of the assassination reached Russia, which was part of the **Soviet Union** and an enemy of the United States in the **Cold War,** radios played funeral music for hours. In West Berlin, at least 60,000 people gathered to mourn the loss of the U.S. president. The square where they gathered was later named after John F. Kennedy.

In Ireland, almost everyone stopped what they were doing to pray for the president and his family. They felt especially close to Kennedy, whose grandfather had come to the United States from Ireland in 1849. In Rome, Italy, taxi drivers parked a taxi outside the American **Embassy** and propped a huge funeral wreath up against it. In England, memorial services for President Kennedy were held all over the country.

The loss of a friend

Telegrams to Mrs. Kennedy began to flood the White House. Everyone from Queen Elizabeth of Great Britain to Nina Khrushchev, the wife of the Soviet leader, sent words of comfort. In France, President Charles de Gaulle watched as his nation mourned. He said, "I am stunned. They are crying all over France. It is as though he were a Frenchman, a member of their own family." In Africa, one man walked ten miles to the American Embassy. Once there, he said, "I have lost a friend and I am so sorry."

MANY THINGS LEFT TO DO

David Ormsby-Gore, the British **ambassador** to the United States, wrote these words in a letter to Robert F. Kennedy after the assassination. He refers to President Kennedy by his nickname, Jack. He wrote, *"Jack was the most charming, considerate, and loyal friend I have ever had, and I mourn him as though he were my own brother. He still had great things to do and he would have done them. Mankind is infinitely poorer."*

In West Berlin, people quietly walked through the streets on the night of November 23rd carrying torches to mourn Kennedy's death.

The Investigation

The Warren Commission

On November 29, 1963, President Johnson assigned a group to study Kennedy's **assassination.** U.S. **Supreme Court** Justice Earl Warren was the head of the **commission.** The group was told by President Johnson to study everything they could about the assassination to find out whether anyone besides Lee Harvey Oswald could have been involved. They were also told to find out more about Jack Ruby's murder of Oswald. Everything was to be reported back to the president and the American people.

Members of the Warren Commission handed their lengthy report to Lyndon Johnson in a formal meeting.

The Warren Report

The members of the commission interviewed 552 witnesses. On September 24, 1964, the commission delivered its report to President Johnson. They concluded that Oswald and no one else was involved in President Kennedy's assassination. There was no **conspiracy,** they said. Many Americans disagreed with the published report. They saw many things in the report that did not seem to be explained by the commission's findings.

Conspiracy theories

Many people wondered if President Kennedy's assassination was the result of a conspiracy. Some people thought organized crime groups might be involved. After all, Robert F. Kennedy—the president's brother and attorney general of the U.S.—was trying to get rid of the Mafia crime ring in the United States. Both Jack Ruby and Oswald had connections to people in the Mafia. Not only that—Oswald had lived and worked for a while in the **Soviet Union,** and his wife was Russian.

Other people thought Fidel Castro might have had something to do with the assassination. Perhaps, they thought, he was getting back at Kennedy for the Bay of Pigs invasion and for the Cuban Missile Crisis. Still others wondered if Americans who hated Kennedy's **liberal** ideas might be involved. Many Southerners, in particular, did not like Kennedy's proposal for **civil rights legislation** that would give African Americans equal rights.

The Select Committee on Assassinations

There were so many questions left unanswered that thirteen years later, in 1977, **Congress** formed another committee, called the Select Committee on Assassinations. Members spent two years going over the Warren Report and interviewing the witnesses who were still alive. They also used more up-to-date technology to study bullets and a tape recording made during the motorcade. This committee announced in 1979 that the evidence did indeed suggest the presence of a second gunman. They did not name any suspects.

Little did Abraham Zapruder know that the film he would take of Kennedy smiling and waving from the Dallas motorcade would become one of the most famous pieces of film in history.

THE ZAPRUDER FILM

On the day President Kennedy was to come to Dallas, Abraham Zapruder, a dress manufacturer, went to see him and took along his movie camera. Zapruder was standing near the schoolbook warehouse and filmed the motorcade as President Kennedy was shot. When investigators found out about the film, they took it. Later, the Warren Commission studied it frame by frame to see if it could help them solve the mystery of what had happened. The film helped investigators time the shots and also helped them to determine exactly where the president's limousine was when the shooting took place.

Innocence Lost

When John F. Kennedy became president, a new decade was beginning, and Americans saw him as a leader who was ready to guide the country into a new frontier. Many Americans planned to vote for him in 1964 to give him the opportunity to lead the country for four more years. The new **civil rights** bill he had presented to **Congress** gave them hope that he was on his way to carrying out the goals of his New Frontier **platform.**

President Kennedy was building up U.S. forces to fight in the war between North and South Vietnam.

His death, however, took away much of that hope. Many historians say that with Kennedy's **assassination,** the whole country lost its innocence. Instead of living in an exciting place where **reforms** were being made, Americans were suddenly living in a country where a president could be killed.

The president's assassination made Americans look at many things differently. When the Warren **Commission's** report was published, people began to question their government in a way they had not before. They began to wonder if the government was keeping information from the public to serve its own interests.

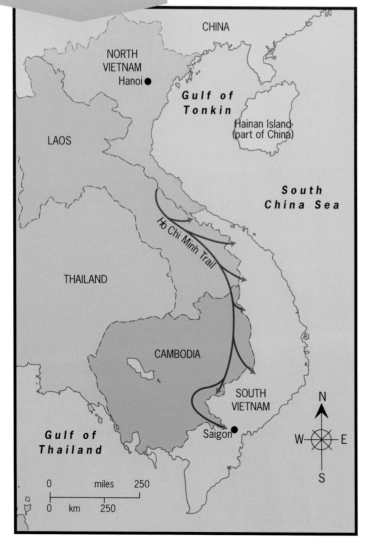

The Vietnam War

Americans also questioned the actions of their country when the government started sending American soldiers to Vietnam. Presidents Eisenhower and Kennedy had both been involved in **negotiations** with Vietnam, but by the time Johnson became president, things were much worse there.

Robert F. Kennedy, shown here at a press conference, was a prominent political figure like his brother John.

American soldiers were sent to fight against North Vietnam, a **communist** country being supported by the **Soviet Union.** The North Vietnamese were moving into South Vietnam, which was not a communist country, and trying to take it over. The United States government did not want to see South Vietnam become a communist nation.

Many Americans protested against U.S. involvement in Vietnam. However, by 1965, the United States had sent more than 180,000 soldiers to fight in South Vietnam. Before the war ended in 1973 with the surrender of South Vietnam to North Vietnam, the war had cost the United States about $200 billion, and about 58,000 Americans had died there.

MORE ASSASSINATIONS

In 1968, Americans were again shocked when two more leaders who had pursued the goals of Kennedy's New Frontier were assassinated. On April 4, 1968, an **assassin** in Memphis, Tennessee, killed Martin Luther King Jr., the best-known civil rights leader of his time. A few months later, on June 5, 1968, John F. Kennedy's brother Robert was shot and killed in Los Angeles, California. At the time, Robert Kennedy was running for president.

Johnson's Presidency

The Great Society

On November 27, 1963, just five days after President Kennedy was **assassinated,** Lyndon B. Johnson gave his first speech to **Congress** as president. Johnson told Congress and America that he wanted to see Kennedy's civil rights bill passed, saying, "Let us continue the ideas and the ideals" of President Kennedy. Johnson had a hard time getting the Senate to pass the bill, but he worked hard, and the Civil Rights Act of 1964 became law on July 2, 1964.

While Kennedy had called his political **platform** the New Frontier, President Johnson won the 1964 election on a platform called the Great Society. Many of the goals of the New Frontier were included in the Great Society, including improved conditions in cities, an end to poverty, and more money for education.

Johnson's vision was of a country where government helped people to help themselves. During his time in office, he established programs to do that.

Giving people a head start

President Johnson and his **cabinet** set up programs to help people get jobs and the Head Start program to help young children from poor homes. Johnson also proposed a law in 1965 to guarantee voting rights for African Americans. Another act, the **Civil Rights** Act of 1968, sought to end racial **discrimination** in the sale or rental of houses or apartments. The laws helped, but the country was still experiencing racial **unrest.** As races clashed, riots broke out in cities such as Detroit, Chicago, and New York.

The war in Vietnam

The Vietnam War continued to be a problem for President Johnson. By 1968, more than 500,000 U.S. troops were in South Vietnam. The war had divided the country, and those who were against the war protested regularly. As time passed and the war continued, more and more Americans began to wonder what would happen next. In 1968, Johnson surprised many by announcing that he would not run for reelection. He said that he felt he had become a symbol for the war, and that perhaps a new leader would find a way out of it.

THE CIVIL RIGHTS ACT OF 1964

The Civil Rights Act proposed by President Kennedy in 1963 and made law in 1964 states the following: *"All persons shall be entitled to the full and equal enjoyment of the goods, services, facilities, privileges, advantages, and accommodations of any place of public accommodation, as defined in this section, without discrimination or segregation on the ground of race, color, religion, or national origin."* It goes on to explain in detail that people may not be discriminated against in theaters, restaurants, hotels, motels, or other public places. Its goal was to establish the Great Society that the United States was meant to be.

Johnson's Great Society provided more opportunities for many people. When Americans think of the 1960s, though, they often do not think of the accomplishments of Kennedy or Johnson. Instead, they recall the shocking assassination of a beloved president, a much-debated war in Vietnam, and a decrease in the nation's wealth and sense of security.

Historians disagree as to whether U.S. involvement in the Vietnam War would have been any different if Kennedy had not been assassinated.

The Kennedy Legacy

Kennedy died without achieving all the goals of his New Frontier **platform.** Some of the goals were later pursued by Johnson. During Kennedy's **inauguration,** Kennedy recognized that it would take a long time to fulfill his promises. He said:

> All this will not be finished in the first hundred days. Nor will it be finished in the first thousand days, nor in the lifetime of this Administration, nor even perhaps in our lifetime on this planet. But let us begin.

Those words gave great hope to many Americans. They wanted to see a changed world—a world of peace, where there was no more poverty and where all people were treated equally under the law. Kennedy knew it would not be easy and that it would take time to make that world.

In a proud moment in U.S. history, Astronaut Buzz Aldrin stood on the moon next to an American flag.

Man on the moon

One of Kennedy's goals has been achieved, perhaps in more ways than he ever thought possible. In a speech he gave on September 12, 1962, President Kennedy told an audience at Rice University in Houston, Texas, that one of his goals for the country was to begin an exploration of space. In his speech that day, he said:

This generation does not intend to founder in the backwash of the coming age of space. We mean to be a part of it—we mean to lead it. For the eyes of the world now look into space, to the moon and to the planets beyond, and we have vowed that we shall not see it governed by a hostile flag of conquest, but by a banner of freedom and peace.

The American space program moved quickly. Two milestones had already occurred in Kennedy's lifetime. On May 5, 1961, Alan Shepard had become the first American to go into space. On February 20, 1962, John Glenn had become the first American to orbit Earth. Several years later, on July 20, 1969, *Apollo 11* astronauts Neil Armstrong and Edwin E. "Buzz" Aldrin Jr. walked on the surface of the moon.

Increased awareness

The **assassination** of President John F. Kennedy seemed to shake Americans out of a kind of sleep. In the years following his death, people began to look at their world in a less innocent, more realistic way. They became more aware of the financial hardships of others, of injustices in society, and what government could do about such problems. Kennedy had not been able to pursue his ideal of a New Frontier, but Americans were now more aware that they had the power to create a government that would achieve the goals that were important to them.

Many places have been named after Kennedy to help people remember him. This is the John F. Kennedy Center for the Performing Arts in Washington, D.C.

Important Dates

1917	May 29	John F. Kennedy born in Brookline, Massachusetts
1940		Kennedy graduates from Harvard University
1941	December 7	Japanese attack Pearl Harbor in Hawaii; United States declares war on Japan on December 8 and enters World War II
1943	August 2	Kennedy's PT boat is cut in two by a Japanese ship; Kennedy is injured, but leads crew to safety
1945	August 6	United States drops nuclear bomb on Hiroshima, Japan
	August 14	Japan surrenders to United States, ending World War II
1946		Kennedy runs for **Congress** and wins
1952		Kennedy runs for U.S. Senate and wins
1953	September 12	Kennedy marries Jacqueline "Jackie" Bouvier
1957		Pulitzer Prize awarded to Kennedy for *Profiles in Courage*
1958		Kennedy reelected to Senate
1960		Democratic Party **nominates** Kennedy for president; Kennedy elected 35th U.S. President
1961	January 20	Kennedy inaugurated
	April 12	Soviet Yuri A. Gagarin becomes first man in space
	April 17	Bay of Pigs invasion fails
	May	Freedom Riders go to Montgomery, Alabama
1962	October	Cuban Missile Crisis
1963	July	Limited Nuclear Test Ban Treaty signed by Soviet Union, Great Britain, and the United States
	August 28	More than 200,000 persons hold a Freedom March in Washington, D.C.
	November 22	President Kennedy assassinated in Dallas, Texas; Lyndon B. Johnson becomes president
	November 24	President's **assassin,** Lee Harvey Oswald, shot and killed by Jack Ruby
	November 25	President Kennedy's funeral
1964	July 2	Kennedy's **Civil Rights** bill passed by Congress
	September 24	Warren **Commission** reports that Oswald acted alone in assassinating the president
1965		United States starts sending troops to Vietnam
1968	April 4	Martin Luther King Jr. assassinated in Memphis, Tennessee
	June 5	Robert Kennedy assassinated in Los Angeles, California
1969	July 20	American Neil Armstrong is first man to walk on the moon
1979		Select Committee on **Assassinations** reports that the assassination probably involved at least two gunmen

Glossary

ambassador   representative sent from one country to another

assassin   person who murders a political figure

assassination   murder of a political figure

boycott   refusal to do business with or engage in other activities with a person, business, organization, or government

cabinet   group of advisers

campaign   course of action one takes to get votes

Central Intelligence Agency (CIA)   U.S. government agency that collects information about the activities of criminal and terrorist groups around the world

civil rights   rights of personal liberty guaranteed to U.S. citizens by the Constitution and by acts of Congress

Cold War   dispute between Western countries and Eastern Europe after World War II, in which they were political enemies but not actually at war

commission   group assigned to a specific duty

communist   person or state that follows a class-free system in which land and industry are owned by the state; follower of communism

Congress   U.S. governing body that makes and changes laws and decides how to spend government money; composed of the U.S. Senate and the House of Representatives

conspiracy   secret plot to achieve a goal

debate   formal discussion before a monitor that follows certain rules of procedure

democracy   type of government in which leaders are elected by the people

desegregate   stop separating people based on race

discriminate   treat someone a particular way because of his or her race, religion, gender, or another characteristic

embassy   building in which ambassadors to another country have offices while they are in a host country

enforce   make sure a rule or law is obeyed

exile   person who had to leave his or her country

federal   from or associated with the United States government

inauguration   ceremony held to swear someone into an office

legislation   act of making laws; or, laws that are made

liberal   open-minded, favoring reforms and progress

minimum wage   smallest amount of money that can be paid to an employee legally

naval blockade   ships from a navy blocking entrance to a country's main ports to keep goods or people from reaching a place

negotiation   process of discussion and compromise with another party to achieve a goal

nominate   name a person who will run for office

platform   plan of action to achieve a goal

popular vote   vote of the citizens of a country

radioactive fallout   dangerous particles that come out of nuclear bombs

reform   change from one policy to another, or any change in a policy

Secret Service   division of U.S. Treasury Department whose members protect the president and his family, among other duties

segregate   separate or set apart by race or gender

Soviet Union   former collection of states in Eastern Europe, led by Russia; also called the USSR

Supreme Court   highest court in U.S. legal system

unconstitutional   something that goes against the U.S. Constitution

unrest   protests, rioting, or other disturbances

Further Reading

Downing, David. *John F. Kennedy*. Chicago: Heinemann Library, 2001.

Joseph, Paul. *John F. Kennedy*. Minneapolis: ABDO Publishing Company, 2000.

Spencer, Lauren. *The Assassination of John F. Kennedy*. New York: Rosen Publishing Group, 2001.

Index